M000289466

DISCARD

CLOSER LOOK AT

OCEANS

Brian Hunter Smart

COPPER BEECH BOOKS
Brookfield, Connecticut

PUBLIC LIBRARY
EAST ORANGE, NEW JERSEY

j 551.46   9/99
cop. 1

© Aladdin Books Ltd 1997
Designed and produced by
Aladdin Books Ltd
28 Percy Street
London W1P 0LD

First published in the United States
in 1999 by
Copper Beech Books,
an imprint of
The Millbrook Press
2 Old New Milford Road
Brookfield, Connecticut 06804

Editor
Michael Flaherty

Designer
Gary Edgar-Hyde

Picture Research
Brooks Krikler Research

Front cover illustration
Gary Edgar-Hyde

Illustrators
Aziz Khan
Simon Girling and Associates
Norman Weaver
Roy Coombs
Guy Smith
David Burroughs
Ian Moores
Gary Edgar-Hyde

Certain illustrations have appeared in
earlier books created by Aladdin Books.

Printed in Belgium
All rights reserved

Library of Congress Cataloging-in-Publication Data
Smart, Brian Hunter
Oceans / by Brian Hunter Smart
p. cm. — (Closer look at)
Includes index.
Summary: Explores the oceans of the world, discussing their floors,
canyons, mountains, volcanoes, movements, storms, and plant and
animal life.
ISBN 0-7613-0903-9 (lib. bdg.)
1. Oceanography—Juvenile literature. 2. Ocean—Juvenile literature.
[1. Ocean. 2. Oceanography.] I. Title. II. Series: Closer look at
(Brookfield, Conn.)
GC21.5.S6   1999   98-47320
551.46—dc21   CIP AC

5 4 3 2 1

20.90
1/22/99

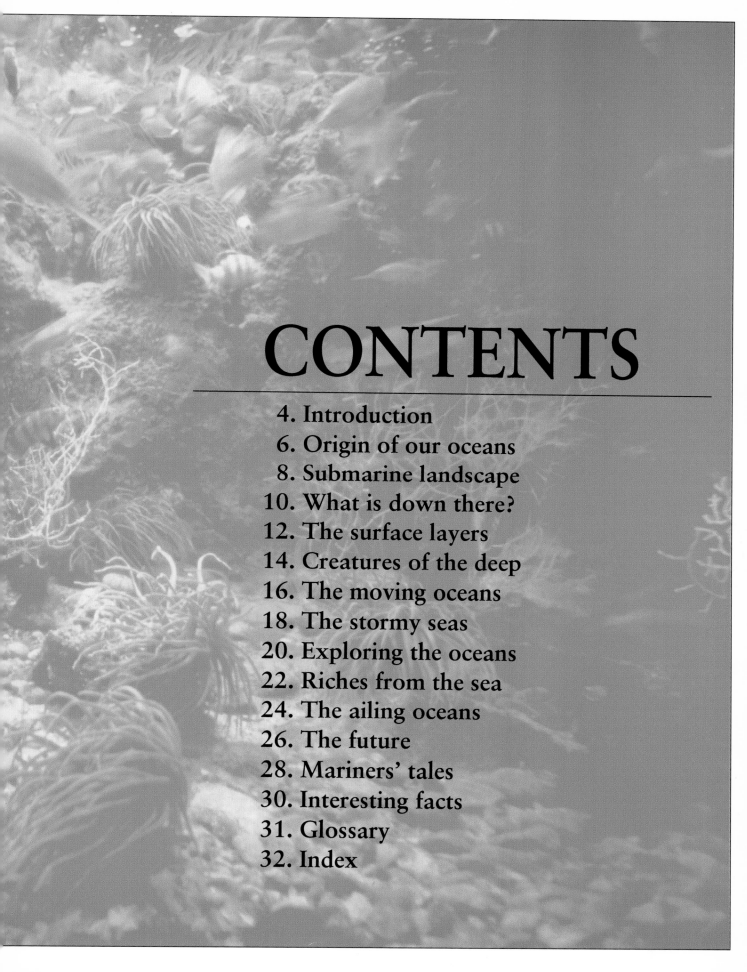

CONTENTS

INTRODUCTION

The oceans cover about three-quarters of the earth's surface. Volcanoes, mountains, and huge canyons spread across the ocean floor in a vast, dark, and largely uncharted underwater world. They teem with many kinds of plant and animal, from tiny plankton and shrimps to giant squid and gigantic whales. Sometimes peaceful, sometimes violent, the seas and oceans will always be a great source of beauty, wonder, and mystery.

Water world

In the last 30 years we have been able to look at pictures of our world from space. The picture below is a view of Earth. The vast expanses of blue are the Pacific (left) and Atlantic (right) Oceans. They give a good impression of how much of the planet's surface is covered with water.

Our planet looks blue from space because much of the surface is covered with water. Most of the world's water is found in the seas and oceans. Only three percent of the water on Earth is "fresh." This includes the glaciers, rivers and lakes, underground springs, and water vapor in the atmosphere.

ORIGIN OF

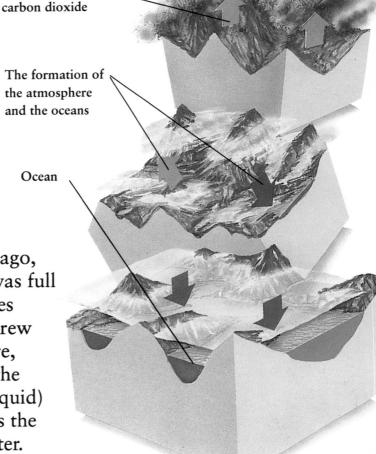

Water vapor and carbon dioxide

The formation of the atmosphere and the oceans

Ocean

THE BARREN EARTH

When Earth formed millions of years ago, it was very hot, and the atmosphere was full of dust and poisonous gases. Volcanoes marked its surface. Their eruptions threw much water vapor into the atmosphere, forming clouds. As the earth cooled, the clouds condensed (turned back into liquid) and fell as rain. Over millions of years the seas and oceans filled up with rainwater.

The original landmass Pangaea was surrounded by an ocean called Panthalassa. Slowly the landmasses moved apart. Today the Pacific Ocean is the largest ocean and is bigger than the Atlantic and Indian Oceans combined.

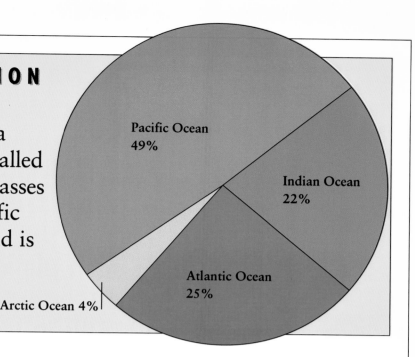

Pacific Ocean 49%

Indian Ocean 22%

Atlantic Ocean 25%

Arctic Ocean 4%

OUR OCEANS

MOVING PLATES

About 200 million years ago Earth had one large area of land, which scientists call Pangaea. Over millions of years, this landmass was pulled apart by movements of Earth's crust, which is split into huge sections called plates. The plates are still moving. Some oceans are expanding (for example, the Atlantic, by 1½ inches (4 cm) per year) and some are shrinking, like the Pacific Ocean.

Water (96.5%)

Sodium chloride (salt) (3%)

Other minerals (0.5%)

Sea soup
Our seas contain water and many types of salts, minerals, plants, and animals. The salt in 1 quart (1 liter) of seawater amounts to about 1.2 ounces (35 g), four-fifths of which is sodium chloride, or common salt. There are also sulfates, calcium, potassium, and magnesium. The seas also contain traces of every element on Earth, including gold!

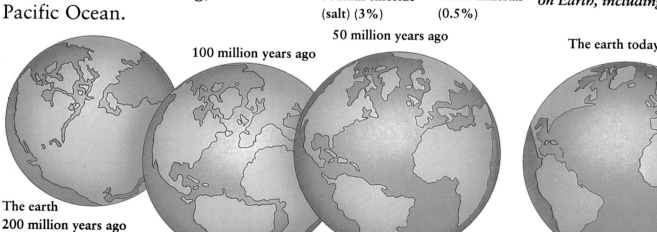

100 million years ago

50 million years ago

The earth today

The earth 200 million years ago

Highs and lows

The highest point on Earth is Mount Everest. The deepest point of the sea floor is the Marianas Trench. The average height of the surface of the earth from the highest peak to the deepest ocean trench is 1.2 miles (2 kilometers) below the surface of the sea.

At certain plate boundaries under the oceans, new oceanic crust is being made. At other boundaries, old crust is disappearing back into the earth. At the fringes of the Pacific Ocean are some of the deepest places on Earth. It is at such places that the old crust is destroyed. Some of this crust is as much as 200 million years old.

SUBMARINE

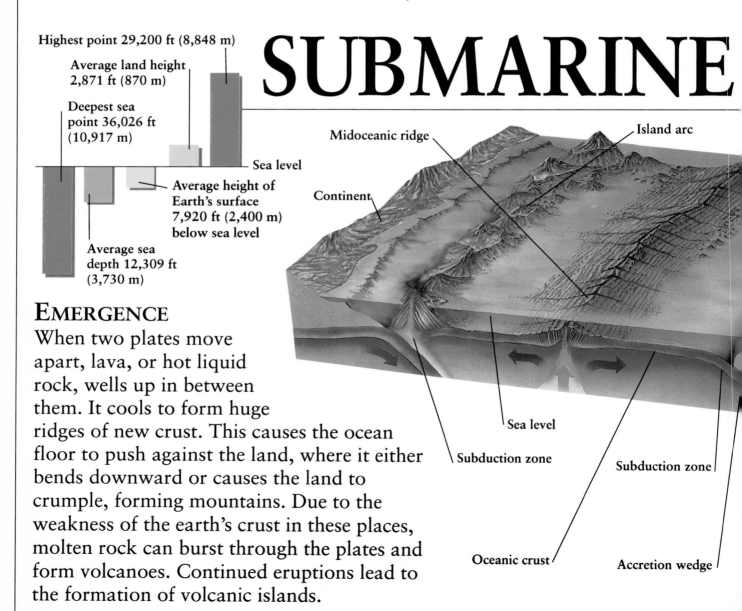

Highest point 29,200 ft (8,848 m)

Average land height 2,871 ft (870 m)

Deepest sea point 36,026 ft (10,917 m)

Average height of Earth's surface 7,920 ft (2,400 m) below sea level

Sea level

Average sea depth 12,309 ft (3,730 m)

Midoceanic ridge

Island arc

Continent

Sea level

Subduction zone

Subduction zone

Oceanic crust

Accretion wedge

EMERGENCE

When two plates move apart, lava, or hot liquid rock, wells up in between them. It cools to form huge ridges of new crust. This causes the ocean floor to push against the land, where it either bends downward or causes the land to crumple, forming mountains. Due to the weakness of the earth's crust in these places, molten rock can burst through the plates and form volcanoes. Continued eruptions lead to the formation of volcanic islands.

ON CLOSER INSPECTION – *Hotspots*

In the deep oceans are found "black smokers," underwater springs that release minerals in a black cloud of smoke. Giant tube worms live here and rely on colonies of bacteria within their bodies to convert sulfur, which is normally toxic, into food.

LANDSCAPE

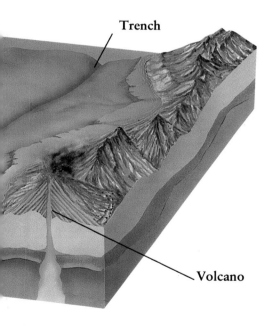

Trench

Volcano

Convergence

When two tectonic plates collide, one plate may be forced beneath the other. This is called subduction and usually involves an oceanic plate sliding under a lighter continental plate. Subduction often creates an ocean trench with a wedge of sediment beyond it called an accretion wedge. Beyond this, a long chain of volcanic islands may form. This is called an island arc.

RING OF FIRE

In the Pacific Ocean, the Pacific plate (below) is surrounded by chains of volcanoes called "Ring of Fire." Most of the volcanoes of the world lie along a few areas, such as around the Pacific Ocean. These areas lie along the boundaries between crustal plates. The map below shows the boundaries between the plates, marked in black.

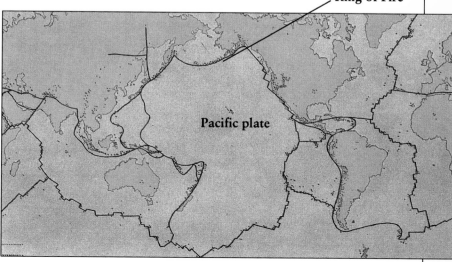

Ring of Fire

Pacific plate

T he seabed is not simply a flat, featureless plateau far below the surface of the sea. It has features similar to dry land, but they are hidden deep beneath the waves. The seabed contains slopes, rises, ridges, mountains, volcanoes, and trenches. There are different zones of the ocean, each with specific characteristics and life forms.

Shore life
The sea supports many land animals, like the seagulls above whose main food source is fish.

WHAT IS

SHELVES, SLOPES, AND RISES
Continents end with a continental shelf of varying widths. The major fisheries of the world are found there. The shelves end with shelf breaks and become continental slopes, then continental rises. Together the shelves, slopes, and rises make up the continental margin. Beyond this is the abyssal plain.

Marine zones
The shallow waters above the continental shelf are known as the sublittoral zone. Light reaches this zone and it is rich with life. Beyond the shelf break in the open sea, it is bright to a depth of 660 feet (200 m). This layer is rich in plankton and other marine life and is called the pelagic zone. Below this to the bottom of the continental slope, about 6,600 feet (2,000m), is the bathyal zone. Only blue light reaches this far, but there are many forms of animal life. Below this is the deepest and darkest zone of the ocean. This is the abyssal zone. The temperature is around 39°F (4°C) and the pressure is tremendous, but there are still many animals to be found here.

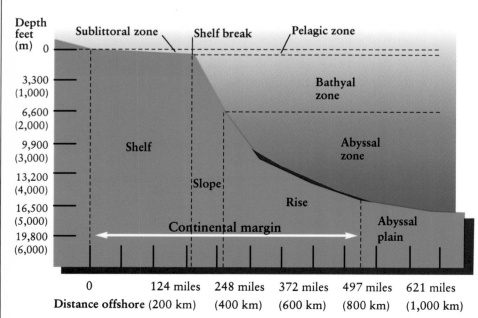

ON CLOSER INSPECTION
– Seamount

The largest seamount is found in the Atlantic Ocean and is called Great Meteor Tablemount. It is 2½ miles (4,000 m) high and over 60 miles (100 km) wide at its base. There are thought to be over 10,000 seamounts and guyots in the world's oceans.

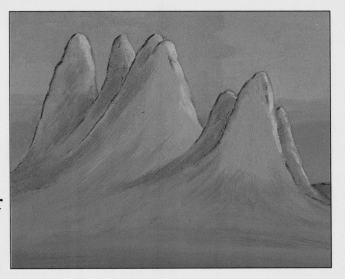

DOWN THERE ?

A guyot is a seamount with a flattened top that forms a plateau under the sea.

Sea surface — Guyot — Seamount — Sea bed — Islands

Profiles of guyots, seamounts, and islands

SEAMOUNTS AND GUYOTS

Underwater mountains are known as seamounts. They are found in all of the oceans. The largest chain, known as the Emperor Seamounts, stretches 3,750 miles (6,000 km) from the Hawaiian Islands to the Aleutian Islands. Guyots are the flattened remains of islands. The largest guyot is 8,910 feet (2,700 m) high. Found in the Pacific Ocean, it is called Pratt Guyot. Guyots and seamounts cause cold, nutrient-rich currents to rise to the surface of the sea, where light penetrates. The nutrients and the light allow plankton to thrive.

The oceans team with life from the bright shallows of coastal waters to the dark, cold depths of the ocean floor. The surface layer, where light can penetrate, supports the widest variety of marine creatures, from tiny animals and plants, called plankton, to humpback whales, which migrate to warm coastal seas to give birth.

THE SURFACE

Reef types
There are three basic types of coral reef. Fringing reefs grow along rocky shores. Barrier reefs grow parallel to the shore, separated by lagoons. Coral atolls are the ring-shaped fringing reefs left after volcanoes have submerged.

THE LIGHT ZONE
Light can penetrate as deep as 3,300 feet (1,000 meters) below the surface of the ocean. Small plants called phytoplankton use sunlight, water, and carbon dioxide to make food. There is only enough light for them to do this down to a depth of 660 feet (200 m). They form the basic food source for other surface dwellers, which in turn are eaten by other creatures. Huge shoals of fish (like the pilchards of the southern Atlantic Ocean) as well as sharks and whales depend ultimately on the growth of these tiny plants.

The shallow waters over the continental shelf are the richest areas of life in the vast oceans.

Dolphin

Jellyfish

Crab

Mackerel

Shark

Angel fish

Turtle

ON CLOSER INSPECTION
– *Small fry*

The seas and oceans are alive with plants and animals from the large to the very small. The smallest of these cannot be seen by the naked eye and are called plankton. There can be up to a million of these creatures in a quart (liter) of seawater.

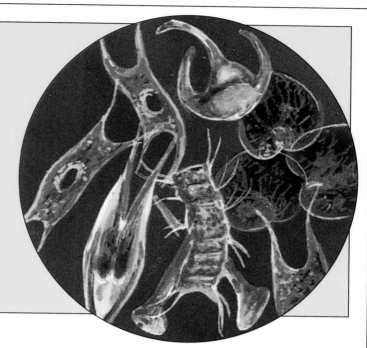

LAYERS

CORAL REEFS

Coral polyps are tiny animals that live together in colonies. They secrete calcium carbonate, which forms a hard, limestone skeleton around their soft bodies. New polyps grow on the skeletons of dead polyps, forming coral reefs.

Marine forest

The coral reefs of the world support a huge variety of life including giant clams, turtles, sea snakes, crabs, and colorful fish of every description. Coral polyps can catch food with their stinging tentacles, but most of their food is made by plant cells that live in their bodies.

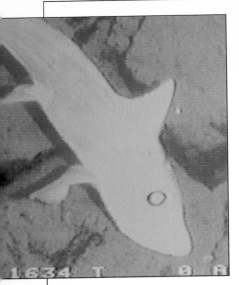

As you go deeper in the seas and oceans, it gets gradually darker, until there is no light at all. In the depths of the oceans there are many weird and wonderful creatures that we know very little about. As we increase our knowledge of the ocean floor, we may discover even more exotic creatures.

CREATURES

Deep divers
Sharks have adapted in many ways to the various conditions that exist beneath the waves. This deep-sea shark, above, lives at the bottom of the sea in total darkness.

The picture at right shows some of the nightmarish fish that live deep in the ocean where light cannot reach.

STRANGE CREATURES

There are animals in the oceans that are very strange-looking. The viper fish can eat things twice its size by widening its mouth enormously and expanding its stomach. The angler fish attracts prey with a spike on its forehead that glows in the dark. The end of the spike contains bacteria that create light. This is called bioluminescence. Many creatures that live in these dark depths produce light by various methods. The lantern fish, viper fish, and photostomias are three other species that produce light.

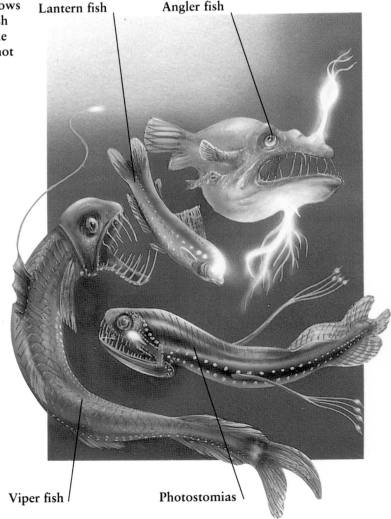

Lantern fish

Angler fish

Viper fish

Photostomias

ON CLOSER INSPECTION – *Coelacanth*

The coelacanth is a very ancient fish, thought to have died out about 600 million years ago. However, in the 1930s fishermen in the Indian Ocean caught one. The coelacanth differs from other fish as it gives birth to live young instead of laying eggs.

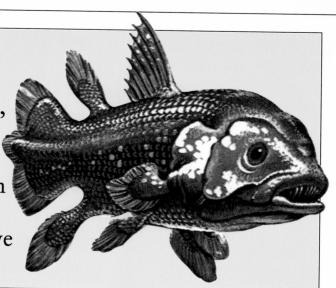

OF THE DEEP

Giant squid

Bottom dwellers
Right at the bottom of the oceans, despite the cold and dark, life still exists. Sea cucumbers, tripod fish, worms (below), and snails all live on the seabed hunting for food. There could be other animals down there, but we just do not know yet.

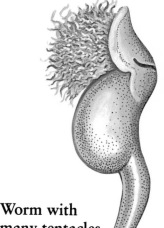

Beard worm

Worm with many tentacles

OCEAN GIANTS

Giant squid can grow up to 66 feet (20 m) long. The largest invertebrates in the world, they have the largest eyes of any living animal, measuring 16 inches (40 cm) across. Giant squid are hunted by Sperm whales. They live far below the surface, so the air-breathing Sperm whale must dive to depths over 990 feet (300 m), using sound waves to locate their prey.

Wave movement

Wind blowing over the surface of the sea causes the water to move up and down in a circular motion (below). Waves out at sea move in the direction of the wind. In wide oceans huge waves develop, called swells. Near to shore, waves get closer together and taller. When the waves get too tall they spill over or break against the shore.

The oceans never remain still. The tides, currents, and waves keep the seas moving constantly. These movements of water are caused by the sun, the moon, the turning of the earth, and wind. These water movements can be slow or fast, but they are important to many of the creatures in the sea.

THE MOVING

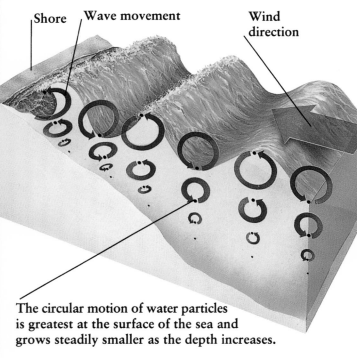

Shore Wave movement Wind direction

The circular motion of water particles is greatest at the surface of the sea and grows steadily smaller as the depth increases.

The world's prevailing winds shape the ocean's surface currents (right). However, the currents are also affected by Earth's rotation and the shape of the ocean floor, which can draw them into giant circles.

➤ Cold currents
➤ Warm currents
➤ Seasonal drift during winter

CIRCULATION OF OUR SEAS

Massive currents called gyres are formed by Earth's rotation. In the Northern Hemisphere they go clockwise, but in the south they go counterclockwise. These currents can be warm or cold and cause

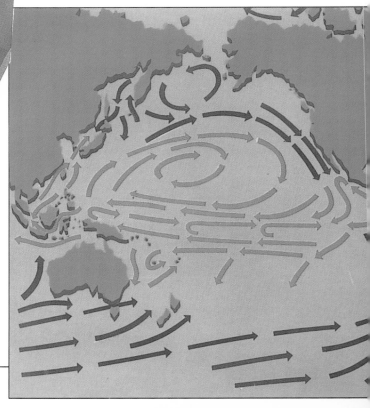

The salts in seawater are more concentrated than those in the blood of mammals. Sea-dwelling mammals, like the beluga whale (right), have adapted to ensure that sea salt doesn't disrupt the delicate balance of body salts.

OCEANS

water to mix globally.

Upwelling occurs when the wind blows away from the land, forcing warm surface water away from shore. Cooler, deeper, nutrient-rich water rises to replace it.

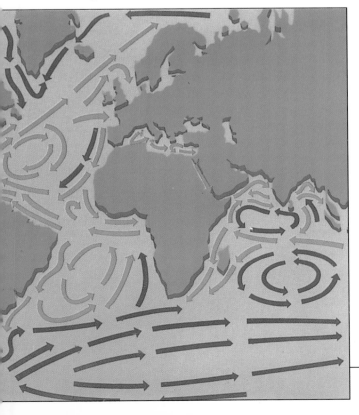

OUR CHANGING TIDES

The sun and moon cause tidal bulges as their gravitational pulls act on the oceans. When the sun, earth, and moon are in a line the greatest rise in tidal levels occur (spring tides) because the sun's pull is added to the moon's; this happens whenever there is a full or new moon. When the sun, earth, and moon form a right angle, the tidal bulges are smaller. Because the sun counteracts the moon's effect, the smaller rise in tidal levels occurs (neap tides).

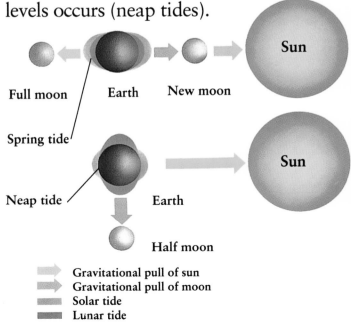

Full moon   Earth   New moon   Sun

Spring tide

Neap tide   Earth   Sun

Half moon

➡ Gravitational pull of sun
➡ Gravitational pull of moon
▬ Solar tide
▬ Lunar tide

The oceans play an important role in the shaping of Earth's weather systems. They help to create some of the most dramatic weather conditions on our planet and are, in turn, affected by them. They can be calm and peaceful when the weather is sultry, or violent and terrible during seasonal, tropical hurricanes.

THE STORMY

Hurricanes

Hurricanes form over warm, tropical seas. They are known as hurricanes in the Caribbean, from the Carib word "hurrican," or evil spirit. In the Indian Ocean they are known as cyclones and in the Pacific Ocean as typhoons, from the Chinese "dai fung," or big wind.

Air rotates and goes up the center of the storm (pink arrows) and then moves out at the top (blue arrows).

HURRICANES

These storms form in the tropics and twist with Earth's spin. Air is sucked in at the base and rises to the top, to form rain clouds. Winds can reach 100 miles per hour. The storms can be 300 miles across.

The eye is the calm center of the storm.

Air is sucked in at the bottom of the storm.

Powerful winds (green arrow) cause the clouds to spin.

Storm surges

Storm winds combined with a spring tide (see page 17) can cause such a rise in sea level that the land becomes flooded. This can cause serious damage to boats, housing, harbors, and coastal farmland.

ON CLOSER INSPECTION – *Waterspouts*

When a spiral of air reaches down from thunderclouds over the sea, it sucks up a column of water that can be 660 feet (200 m) across and 3,300 feet (1,000 m) high. When finally released, this amount of water can be incredibly dangerous.

SEAS

Tsunami

"Tsunami" is a Japanese word used to describe a tidal wave. Caused by an earthquake under the sea, tsunamis can travel at up to 420 miles per hour (700 km/h) across the oceans, but are relatively small. In shallow water, they build up to become huge walls of water over 100 feet (30 m) high.

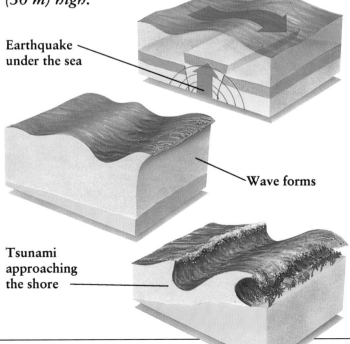

Earthquake under the sea

Wave forms

Tsunami approaching the shore

WHEN IS A STORM NOT A STORM?

Admiral Beaufort, of the British Royal Navy, devised a table to categorize wind speeds at sea (below), known as the Beaufort Scale.

1 Calm — smoke rises vertically.

2 Slight breeze — smoke drifts.

3 Gentle breeze — leaves rustle.

4 Moderate breeze — twigs move.

5 Fresh breeze — waves form small crests.

6 Strong breeze — wind whistles in telephone wires.

7 Near gale — whole trees sway.

8 Gale — it is difficult to walk.

9 Strong gale — tiles are blown from roofs.

10 Storm — trees are uprooted.

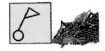

11 Violent storm — buildings are damaged.

12 Hurricane — devastation is caused.

Scuba diving

In the 1940s, Jacques Cousteau invented the self-contained underwater breathing apparatus (SCUBA),

and since then many people have been able to discover what is beneath the waves.

For centuries, people have been fascinated by the oceans. Since the 1600s, we have attempted to explore this watery world using diving suits with metal helmets, diving bells, and scuba gear. Modern submersibles allow scientists to explore ever deeper into this submarine world.

EXPLORING

MAPPING THE OCEANS

Since the 1940s, advances have been made in oceanic exploration. Explorers have been able to go deeper into the oceans with pressurized suits, submersibles, and bathyscaphes, which can descend 6¼ miles (10,000m). Scientists use sonar (sound) to produce pictures of the seabed, while unmanned vessels travel far below the surface to collect samples and take photographs.

Sealink

Bathysphere, built in 1934, can dive 3,052 feet (925 m) deep.

Deep-sea camera

ON CLOSER INSPECTION
– Under pressure
Pressure increases in the sea as you descend. At 6,600 feet (2,000 m) the pressure is almost 2,000 times greater than the pressure at sea level. Divers would be crushed at this depth, so they are protected by pressurized suits or submarine craft such as *Alvin* (right).

THE OCEANS

This diagram shows some equipment used for deep-sea exploration.

Trieste, built in 1953, can dive 6.8 miles (10,920 m) deep.

Tech diver

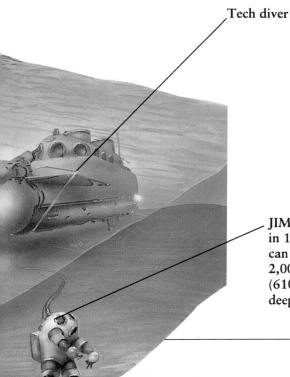

JIM, built in 1971, can dive 2,000 feet (610 m) deep.

WRECKS AND RICHES
Many shipwrecks, sunken treasures, and ruined cities lie on the seabed. Recently, the *Titanic* (below) and the *Marie Rose*, King Henry VIII's warship, have been found and studied. The *Titanic* lies over 2.4 miles (4 km) under the sea, too deep for divers to reach except in a small submarine called a submersible.

The sea has been a source of food, energy, and minerals for thousands of years. Many countries include large amounts of seafood in their diets. It is a rich source of protein and nutrients. Minerals like common salt can be extracted from the sea. Oil and gas are among today's most sought-after resources. They exist beneath the seabed in many places.

Shipping
From the dugout canoe to today's massive oil tankers (above), ships are one of the most important and oldest forms of transportation. International trade relies heavily on ships.

RICHES FROM

SEAFOOD
For centuries, we have fished the oceans close to the shore. Not only fish, but seaweed, lobsters, cockles and mussels, and squid and octopus are taken from the seas as sources of food.

Offshore fishing
Fish are caught in a variety of ways. Individuals can catch fish using fishing rods, traps, or small nets, from the shore or in boats. Groups of people can catch many more fish on boats using trawls, beach seines, or gill nets.

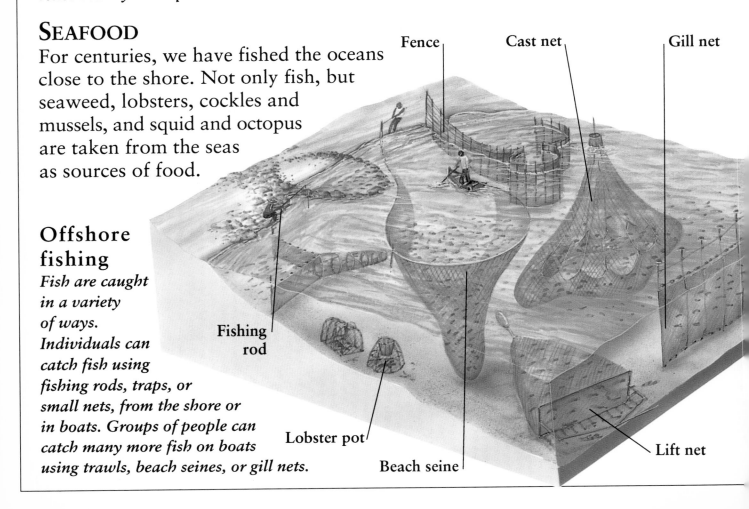

Fence | Cast net | Gill net

Fishing rod

Lobster pot

Beach seine

Lift net

ON CLOSER INSPECTION
– *Manganese mining*

Manganese is used to strengthen metal alloys, like steel. There are manganese nodules in certain areas on the seabed. They grow very slowly, a few fractions of an inch every million years. They could become a rich source of the mineral in the future, but mining them now is too costly.

THE SEA

OIL AND GAS

About 20% of the world's supply of oil and gas comes from beneath the seabed. Oil and gas rigs extract these important resources from the ocean floor. Oil is processed to make gasoline, drugs, dyes, plastics, and explosives.

MINERALS

Minerals such as magnesium, iodine, and bromine as well as salt can be extracted from seawater. Sand, grit, diamonds, copper, iron, and gold can also be mined from the seabed.

The main fishing zones are shown on the map below. Half the fish are caught along the coasts (red line). Main offshore fisheries are shown in blue.

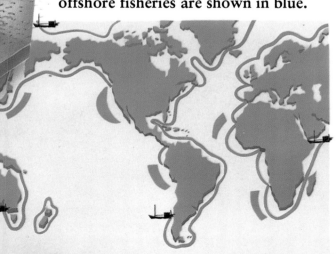

The oceans can tolerate a certain amount of pollution but human and industrial waste can spread diseases to both humans and marine life. Pollution can occur in the oceans by accident, through carelessness, or on purpose. Whatever the reason, the effects are usually disastrous.

Industrial waste

Chemicals, animal and plant matter, and waste water is either piped or dumped into the ocean by barges (above). Billions of tons of waste enter the sea in this way every year; it is a major source of marine pollution.

THE AILING

OIL

Oil seeps into the seas naturally through cracks in the ocean floor, but spills from oil rigs and tankers add greatly to this. The effects of oil pollution on marine life are devastating.

PLASTICS

Marine animals get tangled up in plastic objects such as six-pack can holders, broken nets, and fishing line. These materials do not erode quickly and so their threat lasts for many years.

Spills and leakages from oil refineries

Oil tanker accidents

Discharges from ships and tankers at sea

Leakages from oil pipelines

Leakages and waste dumped from oil-drilling platforms

The seas take a long time to recover from an oil spill. The wildlife is devastated. When oil covers a bird's feathers, they lose their waterproofing. The feathers become waterlogged and the bird drowns or freezes to death.

OCEANS

OVERFISHING

Modern fishing vessels have equipment to help find shoals of fish and two-way radios to keep them up to date with weather conditions. In some areas, fish stocks are decreasing rapidly, because more fish are being caught than can be replaced by breeding. This is called overfishing.

A wasteful process
We take many varieties of fish from the sea. Unfortunately, animals that are not wanted, such as dolphins (left), are caught at the same time or drowned in the nets. Dead, their bodies are discarded into the sea.

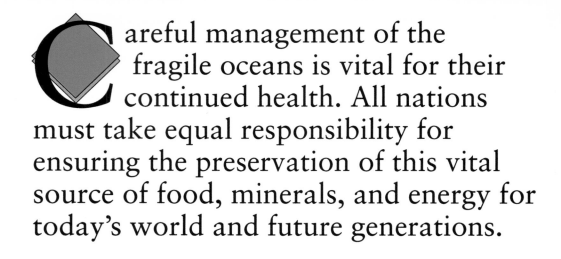

areful management of the fragile oceans is vital for their continued health. All nations must take equal responsibility for ensuring the preservation of this vital source of food, minerals, and energy for today's world and future generations.

THE FUTURE

MARINE PARKS

The development of more marine parks, especially around coral reefs, where the abundance of life is incredible, will have a positive impact on the seas and the life that they support. Marine parks help limit pollution and ban fishing. They therefore provide a safer haven for endangered marine life.

FISHING AND FARMING

Taking care of our fisheries is vital for the survival of many marine creatures. Expanding the types of foods that we take from the sea would reduce the pressure on some fish stocks. A more environmentally friendly alternative to fishing is farming in the sea (above), which is already making an impact on seaweed, salmon, prawns, and oysters.

The temperature of Earth seems to be rising. This may lead to the eventual melting of the polar ice caps. The resulting rise in sea level could flood low-lying coastal areas, cities, and even whole countries. Places like New York and Bangladesh could become submerged by seawater.

ENERGY

Waves and the tides contain a lot of energy. Driven by the wind, sun, and moon, they are continual. Many experiments (see below) are being carried out to harness that energy to drive electric generators. There is also a project to use differences in the temperatures of surface and deep seawater to drive turbines to generate electricity. This is called ocean thermal energy conversion (OTEC).

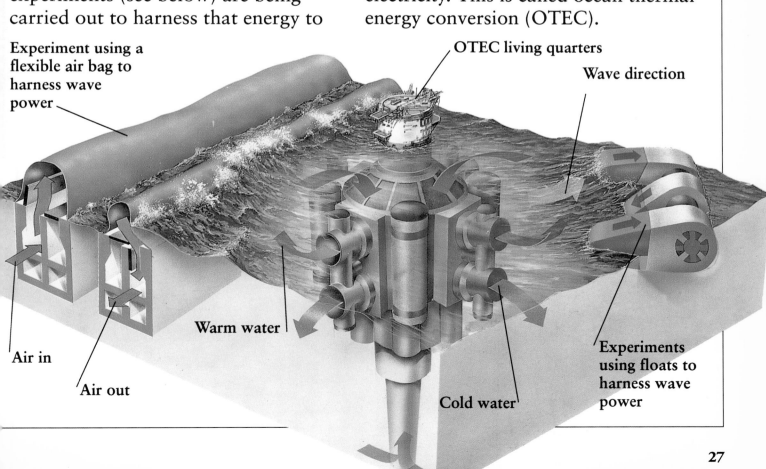

Experiment using a flexible air bag to harness wave power

OTEC living quarters

Wave direction

Air in

Air out

Warm water

Cold water

Experiments using floats to harness wave power

The Bermuda Triangle

More than 70 ships and 20 planes have mysteriously disappeared in this area of the Atlantic Ocean. This includes five U.S. warplanes, which vanished from radar screens in 1947.

Hundreds of years ago people believed that Earth was flat and that you would fall off the edge if you sailed too far from land. They also believed that the deep sea was filled with monsters that would destroy all who were foolish enough to venture far from shore.

MARINERS'

The *Marie Celeste*

This ship was found in the Atlantic Ocean with no one on board (left). The crew had disappeared without a trace. It is still a great mystery today.

The Kraken wakes

Norwegian folklore tells of a terrifying beast that came from the deep, looked like an octopus (below), and would drag a ship and all her crew to a watery grave.

On Closer Inspection – *Manatee*

The mermaid myth may be due to sailors mistaking a sea cow (manatee or dugong) for a woman with a fish's tail. Similar stories have arisen in many different parts of the world.

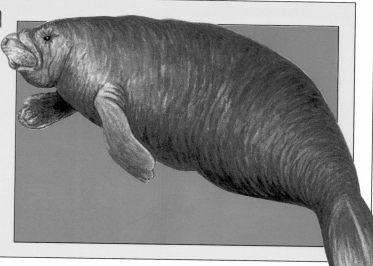

TALES

THE LOST CITY OF ATLANTIS

The lost city was described by the Greek writer Plato (428-348 B.C.) who wrote that the island was engulfed by waves over 3,000 years ago. A volcanic eruption on the island of Santorini in the Mediterranean blew half the island away and caused great tidal waves. This may be the basis of the stories, but there are ruined cities beneath the waves on the Turkish coast that simply slipped into the sea.

SEA SERPENTS

Tales of huge sea serpents could be blamed on the oarfish (above) which can grow to 23 feet (7 m) long. However, sea serpents do exist. There are 50 varieties, and they are among the most venomous of snakes, but they rarely grow more than 6½ feet (2 m) long.

Europe

Santorini

Mediterranean Sea

Africa

The most famous oil spill occurred in Prince William Sound when the *Exxon Valdez* ran aground in Alaska in 1989. The oil that was spilled destroyed much of the marine life along the Alaskan shoreline. The marine life in the area is still trying to recover.

The kraken, from Norwegian folklore, was probably a giant squid. A specimen was beached in Thimble Tickle Bay, Newfoundland, Canada in 1878.

There are over 30,000 types of fish in the world's oceans, yet we only catch around 200 types for food.

Hurricanes hit the southern states of America and the Caribbean in late summer and early fall. Hurricane Mitch, which struck the

INTERESTING FACTS

It weighed 2 tons and was about 55 feet long.

Whales are the biggest creatures in the seas and oceans. Blue whales can grow to a staggering 99 feet in length and can weigh 165 tons. At birth they are already 26½ feet long.

western Caribbean in 1998, had caused the death of 10,000 people by November 2 of that year. It was the strongest storm since Hurricane Gilbert in 1988.

Tsunamis regularly wreak havoc all over the Pacific Ocean. They travel at up to 420 miles per hour and swamp low-lying land. A tsunami struck East Java in 1994 and caused 250 casualties.

The total amount of water in the oceans is 840 million cubic miles (3,500 million cubic kilometers). The polar ice caps contain 12 million cubic miles (50 cubic km) of water. Seventy percent of the world's fresh water supply is frozen.

The many nations that use the seas have different types of ships for different functions. The largest tanker fleet is registered in Liberia. Panama has the largest registry of bulk cargo carriers. The U.S.A. has the largest military surface fleet, and Russia has the largest military submarine fleet.

Atolls These are caused by corals growing on the sides of a volcano that has emerged from the sea. The volcano, worn away by the weather, slowly submerges, and a ring of low-lying coral islands, or atolls, are left.

Black smoker This is a hot, underwater volcanic spring found next to a midoceanic ridge. It releases hot water filled with minerals that looks like black smoke pouring from the sea floor.

Crust The earth's outermost layer that forms a hard shell. The oceanic crust is only between 4 and 7 miles thick. The continental crust is between 18 and 24 miles thick.

Guyot This is a seamount whose summit has been worn away by the waves, giving it a flat top.

Gyre These are massive movements of water caused by Earth spinning on its axis. In the Northern Hemisphere, these oceanic currents move clockwise, but in the southern oceans they move counterclockwise.

Hurricanes These are tropical storms that cause devastation as they move away from the equator. Hurricanes are also known as cyclones and typhoons.

Plankton These are tiny creatures that live in the sea. They can be phytoplankton (plants) or zooplankton (animals).

Plates These are the huge pieces that form the earth's crust.

Ridges Midoceanic ridges occur where two plates move apart and ridges form from the cooling of the molten rock which is forced up from the center of the earth.

Scuba The self-contained underwater breathing apparatus was invented in the 1940s by Jacques Cousteau. It allows people to breathe underwater for a long time but limits the scuba diver to 165 feet of depth.

Sea farming This is the intensive growing of seafoods such as salmon, seaweed, and oysters. This is a very productive process and much better than wasteful fishing techniques.

Seamount This is a mountain under the sea.

GLOSSARY

Tides These can be spring tides (large difference between high and low tide) or neap tides (smaller range between high and low tides). They are affected by the gravitational pull of the moon and sun.

Trenches These are deep areas of the ocean seabed that are caused by one crustal plate slipping beneath another.

Tsunami These are very powerful waves that wreak havoc and leave devastation in their wake. They are caused by underwater earthquakes.

Upwelling When the wind blows away from the land it causes water to move away from the coast with it. Cold, nutrient-rich water rises to replaces the warmer water that has moved away, usually producing a good fishery.

Volcano A gap in Earth's crust from which molten rock emerges onto the surface.

INDEX

Photo Credits

Abbreviations: t-top, m-middle, b-bottom, r-right, l-left, c-center

All the pictures in this book were supplied by Frank Spooner Pictures except for the following pages:
5: Roger Vlitos; 6, 17t, 18, 22t, 25: Science Photo Library; 20, 27 both: Mary Evans Picture Library.

EAST ORANGE PUBLIC LIBRARY
Oceans
Jr.Dept. 551.46 / Smart, Brian Hunte

3 2665 0033 8252 2

DATE DUE

MAY 3 2002 **DISCARD**	
JUN 0 3 2002	
JUN 0 4 2002	
JUN 0 4 2002	
JUN 5 2002	
JUN 5 2002	
JUN 0 6 2002	
JUN 0 7 2002	
JUN 0 8 2002	

DEMCO, INC. 38-2931